The Mirror Told Me

**Also In The Series**

**If He Was Mine**

In the first volume of the *When Insecurities Speak Self-Development Series, If He Was Mine,* the author takes the reader on a discovery expedition into the deepest, darkest parts of the individual's soul. *If He Was Mine* is specifically crafted to speak to the hearts, minds, and souls of women who are in search of "the one," their true love, their soul mate. Indeed, many women have fallen time and again for someone whom they barely know. Could the reason be that many women barely know themselves? Have they hidden behind their insecurities for far too long? In *If He Was Mine,* the reader is privy to the thoughts of a woman who perpetually masks her insecurities and seeks to fill the voids in superfluous romantic relationships. In analyzing the daily rendezvouses of the mysterious lady, the author takes the reader on an unforgettable journey to healing so that she—the reader—can ultimately love herself, first, rather than looking for love in all the wrong places. Purchase a copy today; your journey awaits you. Ahoy *soul* matey!

**A Self-Development Series**

**When Insecurities Speak**

**Volume 2**

# The Mirror Told Me

Chakita Hargrove

HeartInk Press

*Since 2008*

Tallahassee • Plant City

© 2011 by Chakita Hargrove

Hargrove, Chakita. The mirror told me/A self-development series/
When insecurities speak/Volume 1
Includes bibliographical references (p. 45).
ISBN: 978-0-9835854-3-5

HeartInkPress
www.heartinkpress.com
Tuned to the beat of your heart
Manifesting dreams and visions

*Printed in the United States of America*

# Insecurity Defined

Insecurity is defined in several ways, which include

1) Lacking self-confidence or assurance --
self-doubting

2) Being the quality or state of insecure,
unstable, or shaky -- instability

3) Being anxious or afraid -- not confident

5) Being inadequately protected

6) Feeling apprehension and uncertainty --
lacking assurance or stability

## Purpose

The purpose of the *When Insecurities Speak* series is to address some issues that women and men face. This series will cover relationship issues, self-perception issues, and blaming issues. Most of the issues discussed in this series are deeply rooted in the lives of women and men, and they either deal with their issues internally or in the secret comforts of their rooms. Some women and men resort to journals and mirror conversations whereas some are able to talk openly with a limited number of people.

As aforementioned, insecurity is not an attribute that is only limited to women. There are many men who are also insecure, especially if they have experienced betrayal or if they perceive themselves to be the lesser individual in a relationship. However, most often it appears that women are the more insecure of the species.

Insecurity is damaging to a relationship especially when it is entirely unjustified. For example, women tend to take baggage from old relationships into a new one and behave as if the new relationship is just like the previous un-dealt with relationships.

While most of us are insecure about something, be it our popularity, intelligence, or looks, we tend to deal with it and get on with our lives. We are aware that we are lacking in a certain department, but we also reassure ourselves that we compensate for it in another area. Insecurity, no doubt, becomes a problem when it is unmanaged and verges on paranoia.

Because insecurities can wreak much havoc in the lives of women and men alike, I believe it is worth examining the problem and getting to the root of what causes the insecurity, just as any paranoia can be traced to certain deep-rooted fears.

Most often, insecurity stems from a basic lack of confidence, a feeling of just not being good enough and not being able to measure up to expectations, more from the person him or herself, than from any external source. Sometimes a woman or man becomes insecure due to severe criticism or when a relationship goes sour.

# Introduction

When insecurities are not dealt with, they can stifle personal development and any healthy start or progression of a positive self-perception. Within *The Mirror Told Me* you will find various questions that will assist you in seeing an awesome reflection in the mirror.

A person's self-perception involves more than a body image; a person's self-perception involves the person's identity. A person's identity is like a portrait: a piece can be relationship status, another piece can be level of success, and another piece can be religious belief.

In *The Mirror Told Me* you will deal with your whole person, your identity and body image. It is very important for you, or any person, to know who she or he is. When a person has no grip on her--or his-- identity, she will allow any and all people to define who she is, and this is one way insecurities are developed. People, women and men, begin to believe that they won't amount to anything, that their complexion is too dark, and so on. It is time for you to take your power back and start erasing the negative attributes that people have placed on you (in your mind).

The unhealthy comparison games have to end. No two people are alike; even twins have differences. Unhealthy comparison games cause people to develop eating disorders, and cause people to accept illegal jobs simply to belong.

Please note that this may not be a book you want to pass around because each question should be answered honestly. *The Mirror Told Me* should be treated like your personal journal or diary; a place where you are able to be honest with yourself and write down your inner thoughts.

I hope that this "tool" helps you develop a better self-perception and that you are able to manage (or get rid of) your insecurities in a healthy manner.

*Chakita S. Hargrove*

**B**efore you dive into *The Mirror Told Me,* please write your own commercial. This commercial should be a depiction of who you are and where you are in life. Nothing should be exaggerated (false). As you work your way through *The Mirror Told Me* you will see the purpose behind writing this commercial.

## My Commercial

_____

_____

_____

_____

_____

_____

_____

_____

_____

_____

_____

_____

_____

_____

_____

_____

_____

_____

_____

_____

_____

_____

_____

_____

# My Commercial

_____
_____
_____
_____
_____
_____
_____
_____
_____
_____
_____
_____
_____
_____
_____
_____
_____
_____
_____
_____
_____
_____
_____
_____
_____
_____
_____
_____
_____
_____
_____

# Self-Perception

_____

S elf-perception is defined as an awareness of the characteristics that constitute oneself--self knowledge. In this segment, dealing with self-perception, we are going to take a moment to examine the concept of the self, which is all the characteristics of a person. As part of the examination the concept of self will be defined, how an individual develops a self-concept will be explained, and the relationship between the self and emotion and how this relationship affects an individual's self-esteem will be discussed. The relationship between the self and behavior and how this relationship affects an individual's self-presentation will also be explained.

Before moving any further, answer the following questions:

**1.** How do you see yourself?

_____
_____
_____
_____
_____

**2.** If you have any negative characteristics, what are they?

_____
_____
_____
_____
_____
_____
_____
_____
_____
_____
_____
_____
_____
_____
_____
_____

**3.** What are some of your positive characteristics?

_____
_____
_____
_____
_____
_____
_____
_____
_____
_____
_____
_____
_____
_____
_____
_____

**4.** Why do you think some people address negative characteristics or attributes of a person before they address or recognize the positive?

_____
_____
_____
_____
_____
_____
_____
_____
_____
_____
_____
_____
_____
_____

**5.** Have you ever recognized that when people try to describe an individual to someone they usually use some perceived negative features (e.g. the heavy-set girl, that dude who has the hairy mole on his left cheek, no not that one...the bowlegged one, et cetera)? Why do you think people describe others that way?

_____
_____
_____
_____
_____
_____
_____
_____
_____

# Self-Concept Defined

Self-concept refers to domain-specific evaluations of the self. Santrock (2007) states that individuals can make self-evaluations in many domains of their lives—family, academic, success, athletic, appearance, and so on. For the purpose of *The Mirror Told Me*, we are going to focus on success and appearance, how the reflection in the mirror affects our emotions, self-love, and relationships.

A person's identity is a self-portrait constructed of many pieces, for instance:

1) The vocational or career identity of the individual, where the individual chooses to work, and how he or she gets there.

2) The political standings of the individual, whether liberal, conservative, or balanced.

3) The religious identity of the individual, which is the spiritual beliefs of a person.

4) The relationship status (e.g. single, married, divorced, and so on) of an individual also serves as a piece of an individual's identity.

5) The level to which a person is motivated to be successful (achieve) and is intellectual serves in evaluating the self.

6) The sexual identity (heterosexual, homosexual, or bisexual) of an individual is also a piece of the self-portrait.

7) The ethnical and cultural identity, the part of the world or country the person is from and how intensely the person identifies with his or her cultural heritage plays a major role in the individual's self-concept.

8) The individual's interests (e.g. music, hobbies, sports, et cetera).

9) The individual having an introverted or extraverted personality or having calm, hostile, et cetera characteristics.

10) The individual's physical identity, which is his or her body image.

Please note that the above listed identities are not all identities that affect or define an individual.

Fiske (2010) states, "with the use of a cognitive approach, studying the self has overwhelmingly focused, lately, on the content of people's knowledge of themselves or beliefs about themselves" (Fiske, 2010, p. 180). What people perceive themselves to be is what they truly believe, and it is very difficult to tell them otherwise.

What I would like to accomplish in *The Mirror Told Me* is to have every individual realize that even though he or she looks different from others, he or she is also so beautiful. Indeed it is their--your--differences that make them unique and incomparable to others.

Before moving forward, let's work on your self-portrait. Take a moment and identify yourself below.

**1.** Vocation/Career identity:

_____
_____
_____

**2.** Political standings:

_____
_____
_____

**3.** Religious identity:

_____
_____
_____

**4.** Relationship status:

_____

_____

_____

**5.** Level of Success:

_____

_____

_____

**6.** Sexual identity:

_____

_____

_____

**7.** Ethnical and cultural identity:

_____

_____

_____

**8.** Interests:

_____

_____

_____

**9.** Introvert or extravert:

_____

_____

_____

**10.** Physical identity:

_____

_____

_____

# Developing a Self-Concept

The way that a person begins to develop a self-concept is by first understanding who he or she is. The individual must have a self-understanding, and this requires the individual to evaluate his or her identity.

**1.** Who are you? (Write a brief bio)

_____

_____

_____

_____

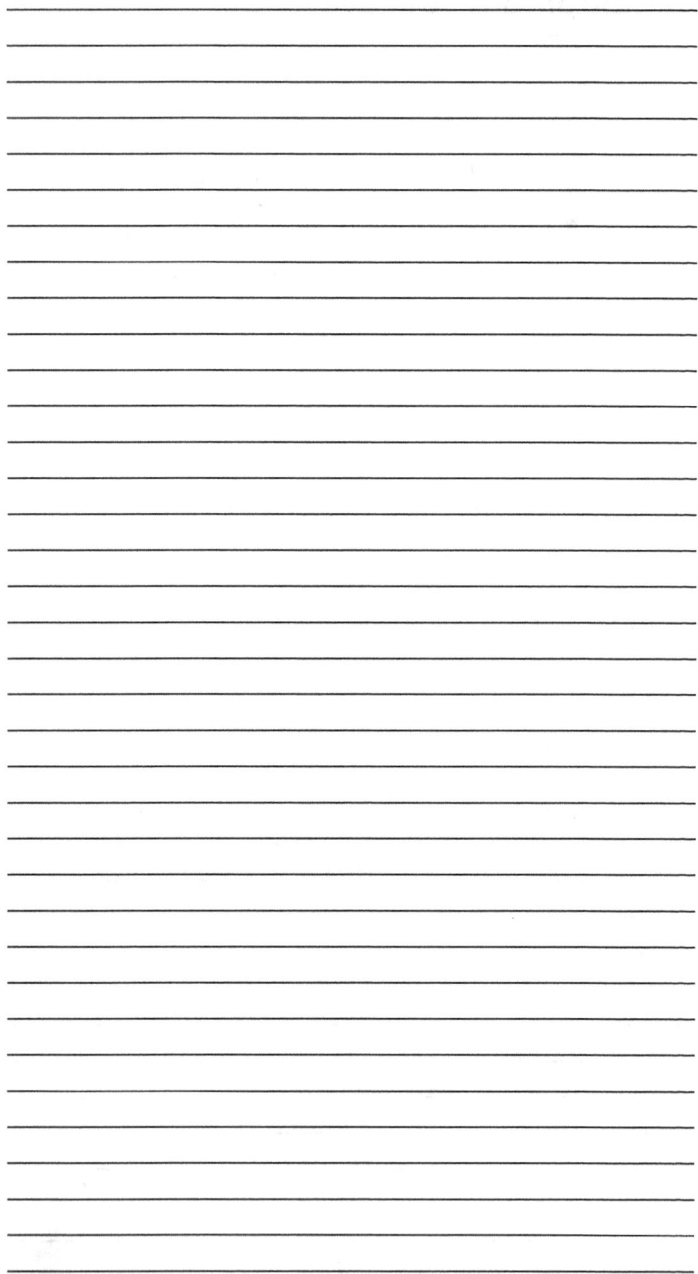

antrock (2007) defines self-understanding as the individual's cognitive representation of the self, which is the substance of self-concepts. Fiske (2010) states that the reason to understand underlies the cognitive of self-concept. He also states that "the cognitive self-concept shows the simultaneous coherence but complexity of the self and how people come to know themselves" (Fiske, 2010, p. 177).

A person begins to know who he or she is once he or she thinks about who *they* presently are by evaluating his or her past and present and looking at what future goals or desires he or she has.

If you don't mind, I would like to have another moment of your time to assist you with developing your self-concept. In the columns below, I want you to write down past goals. Let it also be known if those past goals have been accomplished, if those past goals are still being worked on, and if some past goals have been thrown away. I also want you to write down your present goals, and note whether you have started on those goals. If not, indicate when you will begin. Also list your future goals and desires.

| Past Goals | Present Goals |
|---|---|
| | |

| Accomplished Past Goals | Started Present Goals |
|---|---|
| | |

| In-Progress Past Goals | Start Time of Present Goals |
|---|---|
| | |
| **Canceled Past Goals** | **Future Goals and Desires** |
| | |

**2.** What has caused you to cancel your past goals?

_____
_____
_____
_____
_____
_____
_____
_____
_____
_____
_____
_____
_____
_____
_____
_____
_____
_____
_____
_____
_____
_____
_____
_____
_____

When you get some time, I want you to go back to your future goals and desires and set some dates. Goals are less likely to be accomplished if the target date is constantly moving (is not set).

# Self and Emotion

Once a person learns who he or she is, a reason to self-enhance can occur, especially if the individual does not like what he or she has realized about him or herself. Self-enhancement is a type of motivation that works to make people feel good about themselves and to maintain self-esteem. This motive becomes especially prominent in situations of threat, failure, or various blows to one's self-esteem.

Self-enhancement involves a preference for positive over negative self-views. Self-enhancement is only one of the four self-evaluation motives. The others are self-assessment (the drive for an accurate self-concept), self-verification (the drive for a self-concept congruent with one's identity) and self-improvement (the act of bettering one's self-concept).

When a person learns who he or she is, the person may begin to explain how he or she feels about him or herself. Some individuals, in order to enhance their sense of worth, would downplay the skills that they lack or they criticize others to appear better by comparison. This behavior tricks the individual in believing that he or she has more positive qualities than the next person.

Self-enhancement is found in both types of individuals, those who have high self-esteem and those who have low self-esteem. The difference between the two types of individuals is the strategies of self-enhancement. Those who have low self-esteem avoid situations that would make their negative qualities noticeable.

Fiske (2010) states that one of the reasons people choose to self enhance is because people want to belong. The desire to belong has an effect on self and behavior. Fiske also states that "the affective self shows self-enhancing biases that predict emotional reactions to adverse feedback. And the behaving self shows various forms of strategic self-presentation, self-monitoring, and self-regulating, all designed to gain acceptance by others" (Fiske, 2010, p. 177).

If a person is rejected, he or she may view him or herself as not belonging, which may affect his or her emotions. Adverse feedback is comments or behaviors that are harmful, preventive, and unfavorable. Some individuals aren't capable of ignoring or overlooking adverse feedback, in which that individual's emotions and behaviors can be altered, which could be harmful to the individual and others. The individual can become depressed, develop an eating disorder, or become physically violent towards the tormentor.

Most people have considerably deep reasons as to why they protect the self and the images of the self that they present. People with insecurities worry about social desirability, which is complying with the norms (of a social group or society in general) for responses that reflect positively on one's self. They also resist responding in ways that make them vulnerable to looking incompetent, unkind, dishonest, unfair, biased, and so on.

**1.** Have you ever gone along with the crowd just so you could be seen as being cool? Why or why not?

_____
_____
_____
_____
_____

_____

_____

_____

_____

_____

_____

_____

_____

_____

_____

_____

_____

_____

_____

_____

**2.** Has failure ever caused you to look at yourself in a negative way? Why or why not?

_____

_____

_____

_____

_____

_____

_____

_____

_____

_____

_____

_____

_____

_____

_____

_____

_____

**3.** Did you ever find yourself criticizing another individual just so you could feel better about yourself? How does it make you feel when you constantly critique other people?

_____

_____

_____

_____

_____

_____

_____

_____

_____

_____

_____

_____

_____

_____

_____

_____

_____

_____

_____

_____

_____

_____

_____

_____

_____

_____

_____

_____

_____

_____

_____

_____

**4.** When someone constantly criticizes you and always points out your faults, how does that make you feel?

_____
_____
_____
_____
_____
_____
_____
_____
_____
_____
_____
_____
_____
_____

**5.** What have you ever done to fit in with a crowd?

_____
_____
_____
_____
_____
_____
_____
_____
_____
_____
_____
_____
_____
_____

**6.** What can you do to control your emotions when you feel as though you have been rejected?

_____
_____
_____
_____
_____
_____
_____
_____
_____
_____
_____
_____
_____
_____

**7.** What causes you to protect your image? How do you protect your image?

_____
_____
_____
_____
_____
_____
_____
_____
_____
_____
_____
_____
_____
_____

# Self-Esteem

F iske (2010) states that self-esteem is another area of self-research that focuses on self and emotion. Furthermore, Santrock (2007) states that self-esteem is referred to as self-image or worth and that it is also referred to as global evaluations of the self. How a person sees him or herself and the level of his or her emotional stability can affect his or her self-esteem.

An individual who has a desire to belong, who later experiences rejection, can experience a decrease in self-esteem. A person who defines him or herself by outer appearance can place him or herself in solitude because he or she believes that he or she is not pretty enough. (We are going to talk more about appearance in the next segment of *The Mirror Told Me*.)

There are many factors that could affect (decrease or increase) a person's self-esteem and Santrock (2007) provides five steps that could increase an individual's self-esteem:

1) Identify the causes of low self-esteem and the domains of competence important to the self,

2) Hone emotional support and social approval,

3) Take responsibility for self-esteem,

4) Achieve, and

5) Cope.

Fiske (2010) also states that self-esteem is usually a stable personality disposition and that state self-esteem is much different. State self-esteem is dependent on changes in self-evaluations (e.g. evaluating one's level of success). State self-esteem is looked at as short-term views or short-lived evaluations of the self. People may wake up feeling good but may experience a moment in the day that will alter their self-esteem but later feel good again. Social status, appearance, and much more can affect a person's self-esteem.

**1.** What have you allowed to affect your self-esteem?

_____
_____
_____
_____
_____
_____
_____
_____
_____
_____
_____
_____
_____
_____
_____
_____

**2.** When you are experiencing low self-esteem who are you able to rely on for emotional support?

_____
_____
_____
_____
_____
_____
_____
_____
_____
_____
_____
_____
_____
_____
_____

**3.** How can social approval add harm to your self-image?

_____
_____
_____
_____
_____
_____
_____
_____
_____
_____
_____
_____
_____
_____
_____

**4.** Is it easy for you to cope with change, rejection, and acceptance of who you are? Why or why not?

_____
_____
_____
_____
_____
_____
_____
_____
_____
_____
_____
_____
_____
_____
_____

# Self-Presentation

A person's self and behavior can affect his or her self-presentation. Fiske (2010) states that self-presentation is the final work of operationalizing, which concerns a person's behavior. Self-presentation is how a person portrays him or herself, the identity the individual would like to convey.

People have their own reason as to why they want to portray a certain identity in certain environments. People want to leave a good impression and be seen a specific way that is appropriate for a certain crowd (e.g. presenting themselves as having a lot of money when socializing with business owners).

How a person defines who he or she is will show through the way he or she presents him or herself. Any public failure or embarrassment can cause an individual to showcase a better side of him or her to quickly eliminate his or her shortcoming or bad moment.

How do you present yourself...

**1.** When you are at a job business meeting?

_____

_____

_____

_____

_____

_____

**2.** When you are at work on a normal day?

_____

_____

_____

_____

_____

_____

**3.** When you are among your friends in a public setting?

_____

_____

_____

_____

_____

_____

**4.** When you are among your friends in a private setting?

_____

_____

_____

_____

_____

_____

# My Body

B efore you read further, please take a moment and mark the parts of your body that you do not like or the parts that you think need major improvement.

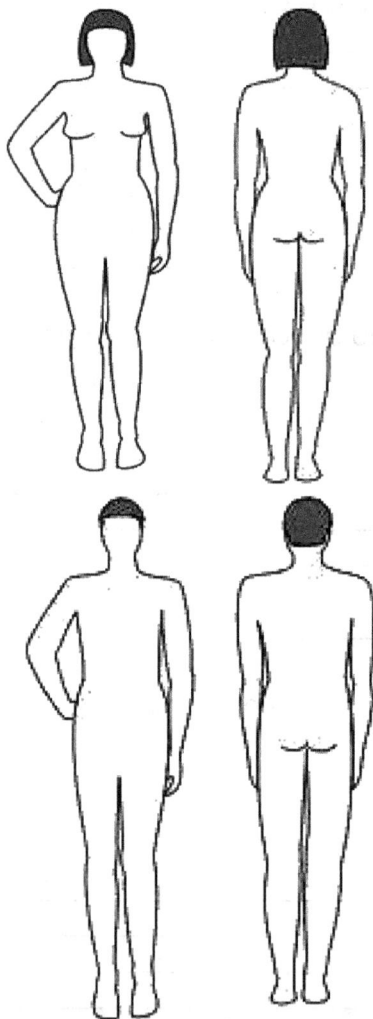

**1.** If any, why do you think that changes need to be made to your appearance?

_____
_____
_____
_____
_____
_____
_____
_____
_____
_____
_____
_____
_____
_____
_____

**2.** Have you ever been criticized or teased about the part(s) of your body you would like to change? How so?

_____
_____
_____
_____
_____
_____
_____
_____
_____
_____
_____
_____
_____
_____
_____

# Body Dysmorphic Disorder

Disclaimer: This section is not intended to aid in a diagnosis. The purpose of this section is to show you how severe an insecurity can become.

Body Dysmorphic Disorder (BDD) is officially classified in the Diagnostic and Statistical Manual of Disorders (APA, 2000) as a somatoform disorder because it involves concern with certain aspects of the body. Individuals with BDD are obsessed with an imagined or perceived flaw or flaws in their appearance to the point that they strongly believe that they are ugly or disfigured. This concern is so intense that it causes clinically significant distress and impairment in occupational or social functioning.

Most individuals who have BDD compulsively check themselves; they constantly check themselves in the mirror or hide or repair a perceived flaw. Individuals with BDD tend to be avoidant of common activities because he or she fears that others will see their imagined defect and be disgusted. In some instances the individual with BDD will lock him or herself up in their home and never go out.

Butcher (2010) states that persons with BDD will focus on almost any part of the body: hair, skin, breasts, eyes, nose, and so on. For example, they may think their hair is too thin, their skin is too blemished or scarred, their breasts are too small, and their eyes are too big. Furthermore, a study found that some of the more common locations for perceived defects include skin (73 percent), hair (56 percent), nose (37 percent), eyes (20 percent), breasts/chest/nipples (21 percent), stomach (22 percent), and face size/shape (12 percent).

It is important to note that people with BDD have concerns about their appearance that is not similar to the ordinary concerns that most individuals have about their appearance; they are far more extreme, leading in many cases to emotional pain and complete preoccupation. In most cases of persons with BDD, the individual sees deformities that another individual may not see. If another individual, or an outsider, does see the so-called "imperfection" the individual with

BDD is referencing, the onlooker may view the "deformity" as minor, but the individual with BDD will, indubitably, see the same deformity as something quite major.

A feature of BDD is that the person will seek frequent reassurance about their perceived defects from their family and friends. However, the reassurance only provides temporary relief. They seek reassurance from themselves by checking their appearance in the mirror numerous times a day (some people avoid mirrors). However, after mirror gazing, they begin to feel worse and so they become excessive with grooming themselves, camouflaging their defect(s) through clothes, hairstyles, or makeup.

What drives people with BDD is the hope that they will one day look different or possibly they will believe that their defect is not all that bad.

# Self-Development and Growth

Before you complete this section, take a moment to review your past answers. If there were any questions that you have skipped, please go back and answer them. The purpose of this section is to build from your self-evaluation. If you have completed all prior questions, let's move on.

Hopefully, *The Mirror Told Me* served as a guide that helped you to overcome some insecurities that have affected your self-perception. It is very important to know who you are rather than letting others define who you are. The main reason why people have insecurities is because of other people. People want to look or have what another person has or they allow the words of others to have power (e.g. power over what they do and power over how they see themselves).

When you look in a mirror you should love the image that is reflected; you should love who you are and how you look. No one should have the power to discredit a beautiful creation.

Everyone looks different for a reason. If we all looked alike, what a "normal" and boring world it would be.

People who have insecurities about their physical appearance resort to surgeries, eating disorders, and isolation. Don't resort to bad (negative) behaviors just to fit-in; it is time to begin to love your-self. If there are any physical attributes that you are insecure about, there are some *healthy* ways to deal with them--the key word is healthy. Please seek a physician or a dietician for those healthy ways.

Now, review all of your answers that you have listed throughout *The Mirror Told Me*. To start the journey to a better self-perception, I want you to take some time and write down or map-out, using the space provided below, how you will begin changing any negative perceptions you have about yourself.

## My Negative Self-Perceptions

_____

_____

_____

_____

_____

_____

_____

# My Negative Self-Perceptions

_____
_____
_____
_____
_____
_____
_____
_____
_____
_____
_____
_____
_____
_____
_____
_____
_____
_____
_____
_____
_____
_____
_____
_____
_____
_____
_____
_____
_____
_____
_____
_____

arlier in *The Mirror Told Me* we talked about goals. I have found that many people make excuses for why they have not accomplished some of their goals. They begin to play the blame game because they don't want to take the responsibility of being their own road block. Often times insecurities are what keeps people back.

No one wants to be looked at crazy for trying something "out of the box," and no one wants to fail. If you want to be successful you have to work for it. Yes, some people are born into families that already have established success, but they still have to work to maintain it.

Change is not a monster. If you don't like your vocation or career identity, your relationship status, or level of success, then begin to work on it. Stop being afraid and explore the healthy ways to change the areas that you can.

Let's set some goals. But first, using the charts provided, list three of your big insecurities. Then, write three personal goals.

| Chart 1: My Insecurities Are... | |
|---|---|
| **1.** | |
| **2.** | |
| **3.** | |

| Chart 2: My Personal Goals Are... | |
|---|---|
| **1.** | |
| **2.** | |
| **3.** | |

Once you have completed the activity above, I want you to think of a "Support Team," a list of trustworthy people who you know will support you in overcoming your three insecurities and pushing you to accomplish your three goals. Using the chart provided, write the names of at least three people you have identified as your

Support Team. You may identify more than three individuals if you like.

| Chart 3: My Support Team | |
|---|---|
| **1.** | |
| **2.** | |
| **3.** | |

Once you have identified your support team, make sure you provide your team members with copies of your insecurities and goals (or you can verbally tell the individuals). Before you give a team member your list, make sure they understand why you are giving the list to them so that they know what role they are to play.

The last thing I want you to do is re-write your commercial: How do you see yourself now that you have dealt with some or all of your insecurities?

## My Commercial

_____
_____
_____
_____
_____
_____

# My Commercial

I hope that *The Mirror Told Me* was a useful tool for you. Please send comments to the author at chakita@freshwindenterprises.com.

If you would like to have the author as a guest speaker, or host a *The Mirror Told Me* session, or if you would like to have a counseling session, please send all requests to
info@freshwindenterprises.com.

More copies of *The Mirror Told Me* can be purchased in the library at:
www.heartinkpress.com

# Certificate of Completion

is presented to

_____

for

Completing The Mirror Told Me volume of When
Insecurities Speak, a Self-Development Series

*Chakita Hargrave, CEO*

_____   _____
Signature                              Date

Fresh Wind Enterprises LLC

## References

American Psychiatric Association (2000). Diagnostic and Statistical Manual of Disorders Fourth Edition, Text revised. American Psychiatric Association. Washington, Dc.

Butcher, J. N., Mineka, S, & Hooley, J. M. (2010). *Abnormal psychology* (14th ed.). Boston: Pearson/Allyn and Bacon.

Fiske, S. T. (2010). *Social beings: Core Motives in Social Psychology* (2nd ed.). Hoboken, NJ: Wiley.

Santrock, J. W. (2007). *A topical approach to life-span development* (3rd ed.). New York: McGraw Hill.

If he was Mine
CHAKITA HARGROVE

SELF-DEVELOPMENT SERIES
When Insecurities Speak:
If he was Mine
Volume 1

www.ingramcontent.com/pod-product-compliance
Lightning Source LLC
Chambersburg PA
CBHW060642280326
41933CB00012B/2123